The Art
of
Waking

Wellstone Press

The Art of Waking

Jonah Bornstein

Wellstone Press

Copyright © 2012 Jonah Bornstein

First edition

*Cover painting: "Wheat Field Under Clouded Sky," (detail)
by Vincent Van Gogh
Cover and interior design: JGB Book Design*

All rights reserved.

ISBN: 978-1-930835-12-2

Published in the United States by Wellstone Press

Some poems included in this collection were originally published in the following collections and anthologies: *We Are Built of Light*; *A Path Through Stone; Treatise on Emptiness* (Wellstone Press); *Deer Drink the Moon* (Ooligan Press), edited by Liz Nakazawa; *Walking Bridges*, edited by Sharon Wood Wortman and Kirsten Rian; and *Jefferson Monthly* (edited by Vince & Patty Wixon)

WELLSTONE PRESS
wellstonepress.com
wellstonepress@gmail.com

For Rebecca Gabriel

Contents

Prelude   11
After A long Rain   12
Looking Out From His Balcony   13
Fall   14
The Art of Waking   16
Tending the Grave   17
Postcard, Taos Mountain Silhouette, 5 a.m.   18
Paper Boat   19
Atheist   20
At the Crematorium   21
First Notes   22
The Bucket Swimmers   23
The Bat Mitvah Party   24
Walking Poem   26
Sea Lion of the Plains   27
Learning To Die   28
In Paradise Answers Rarely Come   29
On A Winter Hillside   30
Trust   31
Of Roots and Dead Fathers   32
Light Comes To The Desert   33
Silent Confession To A Catholic Student   34
Layout Artist   36
Daily Coffee   38
Elegy To My Father   40
Borrowed Fire (A Love Story)   41
After the Trees Came Down   43
Breath   44
Mountain Artery   45

The Flood	46
Where We Stand	47
Dido's Tears	48
Cohabitation	50
Of Breath and Mirrors	52
Untitled	54
Treatise On Emptiness	55
The Verdict	56
Myth	58
A Girl's White Socks	59
Summer Winds	60
The Bird's Wish	62
On the Bank of a Desert	63
Pilot Light	64
Chamber of the Oracle	66
Guest of Honor	68
Elegy for Aryeh	70
Kindness	72
Fertile Ground	73
Another Story	74
Hope	75
The Choice	76
We Are Built Of Light	77
Poem	78
Coda	80

I feel my fate in what I cannot fear.
I learn by going where I have to go.
                    Theodore Roethke, from "The Waking"

Prelude

Go slow. Remember. Build muscle. Do not be afraid. Force yourself to describe, to not let go. Watch fruit bud and bloom, until you can pick it, bite into the succulent beauty of expectation, its sweet juices dripping down your chin into your shirt, onto your chest. Describe the frantic air thrashing and flicking when mosquitoes come too close, the whistles and clicks of birds and insects, the agaves and cacti, penstemons and lilies, the sandstone and limestone, the granite, aggregates, shale, slate—hold them in your palm close to your face, so close that when a breeze brushes the pollens and dust from your hand into the air, they enter you through your mouth, gritty and chalky, through your nose, tickling the hairs that grow as you age, the smell of sweat mixing with it all; then you will understand you are a filter. What enters is the finest stuff and it will mix with you until histories and memories coalesce in your cells and form an intricate web from which nothing is lost.

After A long Rain

And the man looked around him.
He thought of the rain,
how he had tried to hold it in his body, the way it took him
as a virus takes the weak: and he drank of the water
that flowed over him and he never wanted it to end
because there was nothing outside of it.
He was alone and knew no one could ever touch him;
then he thought of everyone he loved
and how they cried
for a river that would flow
always with them
and he saw that everyone mourned in their rooms
just as he mourned, and he saw the rivers flowing,
the fish floating there, their bodies
silent as the leaves that flowed beside them;
and he wanted to hold the people
and whisper to them the way the wind whispers
in trees and grass, the way late and early light
colors the land deep and shallow greens,
to hold them the way the rain held him
but hold on to them as he could not hold the rain,
for it was drawn from him whenever he spoke.
He wanted silence then and companionship,
he wanted to hold the world up and to lie down
in it.

Looking Out From His Balcony

> *Even the linking of the stars is a lie.*
> Rainer Maria Rilke, *Sonnets to Orpheus*, No 11, first series

If he came to die now, the deadfall
of light exhumed from his body
and draped among the trees
of our yard like an old hide
shimmering with frost,

He would choose to be forgotten.

He would render his passion
in the branches of her name
so that she might live, the words
that propelled them into a constellation
of nerves sloughed off each evening
in her bath, their skein of sorrow
unraveling into the wide body

of everything they once longed to be.

He walks into the night, marking his way
down the iced hillside, its mesh of crystal
collapsing under him as an owl blows
westward. Across the sky, the filament
that links the stars flares, then
withers into the creek, which shimmers
silver a moment before plunging
into darkness, a reminder that
it was only beauty they sought

and that nothing is forgiven.

Fall

On the shelf, a girl
sways at the lip of emptiness,
pumps her arm into the twilight
in the madness
of someone exposed too long to mesas
and canyons. I imagine
she is trying to speak to it —
the immensity
daring her to inch out farther than anyone.
Wind ruffles her brown hair,
swells under her arms and falls.

I wonder whether she comes here
often, to touch something
more real than her own life.
She looks across the gorge
toward a country of shadows.
She begins to draw, I think, the underbelly
of the wall's curved heart
swiveling in twilight,
tries to render the emerald necklace bowing
along the canyon floor.
Then a gust that jolts
even the desert-
cast sagebrush lifts
her by the arms and blows her out,
any cry she might make caught
in the wind's throat.
Her knapsack drifts out
from her shoulder, slips away,

rises and quivers
in space
before the current opens
its trapdoor
and swallows it.
I like to think the two ravens
that floated
earlier in the wake
of the invisible
ship of air around her — that their talons
had slit her green sweater, punched
into her flesh to bind the bones
of her arms so that she flew
with them, her weight drawing down
to the canyon floor. I saw

later, the ravens swirl above the rim and knew
she had hovered only, like her pack,
a draft puffing inside her sweater,
so that for an instant she felt the flurry
of being released
into air, its funnel
wrapping her in its body
as she fell toward the mystery she ached to fathom.

The Art of Waking

To rise from sleep,
the days molting from within, to stretch
toward pines circling the lake, with one breath
held beneath reflected spruce, until
there is no ascension from water. Imagine
an exit threaded to the periphery, where cattle turn
to drink from the well of their imprints.
To walk among the desolate and ash
of last year's pelicans, the throb of wings
a memory, where dragonflies whir
locked in heat until they drop,
their faint heart's glow listless
as the pulse of embers. If I could unravel
the brief excess of their mating,
I might step from the circuitry
of sleep, no longer adhering
to disfigured words, the chalky
kiss of love, our binding of earnestness.
Here, no words, no disgrace, as if today
folded back without a name,
no pleasure, but the compass of the body
stretching everywhere, the way a moth begins, squeezing out
from one life into another, more swift and brief.

Tending the Grave
after David Ignatow

If love is to be led
into a forest
to a secret grave
I know what love is.

But what happens
when tending the grave
grows rare, poppies sprout
and fall, petals blow away?

What happens when
the grave grows hard?
Flowers do not bloom,
the shadows of trees turn crisp
and forthright.
There is no one to sing
in the darkness
under the trees.

Postcard, Taos Mountain Silhouette, 5 a.m.

To die
below the moon
its odor waking
prior ruins, when doors
flared their wings
and I walked past.

Moored to desire
the little moon fading,
a blanched sky, and going on,
the yellow-white
mutt of doubt circling,
"Hold on, hold on."

The desert swells,
unfolds its wingless hatch.

I will find a way.

Paper Boat

Last year's skin torn,
fingertips, chest,
eyelids bare as petals;
we touch our flesh with such care,
its remnants strewn like puzzle pieces into the dust,
beneath counters, swept along the days.

Solitude rises
in the rough balls of an old sheet,
rolls across its history every night,
worn and temperate, it knows the peel of blanket,
the opened body a war no longer born.

These places we back into—
a web that holds us still for all to mold.
There is nothing hidden or fought over.
The amalgams of history
dropped in gutters where children hold
the balance, their paper skins pitching
down street toward corners; their boats, brash
with color, stiffen before crumpling under.

We hold our hands before us
as if a new identity might arise
from torn fingers. We cannot look
for what is gone floating away like a receipt.

Atheist
Yom Kippur, 2000

When she came to you that morning
the sun high in the window
of her little house no one had entered
in years, you laughed, pretending to pick sleep
from her eyes, the glow of the television
still thick in corners.
Why didn't you twist
her arm behind her back, force
her to yell out. She didn't have all year.
She gave up playing "queen of the forest" long ago,
the day you put your hands in the back pockets
of your jeans and walked away.

You are a prideful son-of-a-bitch.

Today, she no longer believe in answers. She believes
in light distilled through leaves, the shadow
that traces the pen's rasp, hope that keeps us going.
She believes the picture on the wall
breathes in the paper's nap. And
in the concentrated sadness of everyone,
that nails have a purpose as do coffins.
If you want her to follow when you turn
away you've got another thing coming.

She will find her own way.

At the Crematorium

An artless prophet,
he cranked the handle of his father's
tomb, thinking flame would flower out,
buckle the air with a dismay
that would crease the dull slackness of life.

Faces arced out from the vine like angels,
blurred as the cardboard figures he once bent
around lightbulbs, until switching
the furnace to high, to make
their features glow, delay the rage
that edges the burning of flesh.

He did not know these flaming men,
these women
who bit the air and fell
in blossoms to the slate floor—
their families dispersed to the globe's four corners,
the cold whine that combs through life
a whisper between them.

When the fire dimmed and coals grew dark
he waited—for hands to pat his back, lips to fold
against his cheek, death to withdraw
from the embers, his father's face to uproot
                              the smoke, unravel the air.

First Notes

If a rainbow crossed, igniting
my house, the cedar shingles, tearing
from rafters, tar paper and sheathing
its beckoning yellow and silent indigo collapsing
out of that untouchable girder
of light into our frozen laps,
possibility might strike
the dark chords that pulse
beneath my chin
during sleep, so that its billion pixels tumble
free, all the black hole's swallowings
bursting like a caged flock into the world
until they are lost again, zipped
sweet and snug into this bag
of wakefulness.

The Bucket Swimmers

We drop into the half-bucket of night,
signaling stars to drop their lines when we call.
There is not much to do here as we jostle for space
in the black loam. "Hold us close," say the brothers to the
        fathers,
their voices bouncing against the wooden sides, the fathers
accommodating as they work to keep afloat,
        their smiles of reassurance
tight and angry as they project the future,
the stars forgotten as they begin to swallow splashes of
        blackness.
"Help us father," say the sons and the fathers hold them
        close
in their arms, their hidden desperate kicks buoying them.
"Throw down your light," they suddenly call
        and
the fathers' fear is illuminated, their lobes of silent years
under the chin, their quiet stricken eyes, and they laugh,
all the fathers and sons begin to laugh
        as starlight punctures their skin
and they bloom, their taut skins and eyes,
the night blooming men.

The Bat Mitvah Party

The girl's resistance to prayer unraveled—
the music blared, a bacchanalian release from fidgety hours
stuck before the Haftorah and Talmud, bleary-
eyed like those young Hasids in the rec room shooting pool
after ten hours pecking at nuances of most holy prayer,
                      between shots
tapping their sticks to the sh'ma on the floor, memory fidgeting
in their fingers thin as yads—only when the rabbi unrolled
Moses' five books, the sheep's skin etched
with the new flesh of torah,
had she begun to waver, her story bristling up from the scroll
into her eyes as she learned to read, the wild dancing
she would pursue shifting uneasily in the fibers of her dress
as she maneuvered the thick thoughts
that hung like the universe in nothingness
before it pressure-cooked itself and tore
into what we call the fabric of space,

           which was where she headed
after the last blessing shimmered down the scales of her mind
and began to glide across the floor, one step two steps
                  three, four beats
skimming the shiny floor like a small shoal of being
until it broke when the other girls joined in, kicking,
knocking, thrusting discomfort into dance, the itchy respect
for rabbis and all things other following at their heels
silent as the thoughts of boys strung
along the walls, envying the tight world of girls,
whose shadows glittered under their heels
while they flailed, careening into each other,

hugging pubescence like butterflies gone mad, the boys'
plastic toy-eyes glued to this twisting mystery,
until one fell off a chair, which clattered to the floor,
and the dancers scattered like fish at a small disturbance
before they rematerialized into one body, laughing,
arms flung across each other, remaking the universe,
tumbling together, the one girl's brief beaver shot
bewildering her for just a moment, as she looked wildy
for the boy who might have seen, the adults looking on
invisible, pale humans no more physical than Plato's shadows
dancing in a constellation less real than her own.

The words of the ancient rabbi, the bat mitzvah girl's uncle,
were slung through another line of adults, as perhaps
they were meant to be; take this moment, he said,
                not as a culmination,
but as a beginning of something new, the adults wanting that
clearly, their thoughts reaching into their own lives,
to their youths, how they had ended so many times
and rarely fully taken with them what came before,
but as she danced his words were only a whisper,
fluttering at the window, the cabal of the present
                all that mattered.

Walking Poem

The cedar and the oak

The ponderosa and the madrone

Robin in the sour cherry tree
        Winter
        leaves
the burnt-orange bellies of robins

A Chinese maple barren and bound,
its long neck crooked and craned —
        oh swan —
desire stretching toward me

toe to heel, front to back
        place one foot in front of the other
This, my life
the day's dark
matter moving through me
life passing out
tugging my hand
a spring of what we are
        hiding in our outlines
drifting like fog
across a field
        into this cold day slipping
against a stone, where even a river freezes
against a single stalk before it falls

Sea Lion of the Plains

Cockeyed and stuttering,
we turn to who lies beside us,
slipping inside the flood
of a full body, a scale of sorts,
the body's desire
for the dark pewter of oblivion.

I want to lie down in the hard beads
of transformation where water
loses its body and finds it is more
than liquid, it is the well where souls
dip three times, and blossom in
the forsaken, where people hold their
breath like sea lions of the plains
the very air a cinch on their strangeness here.

Learning To Die

Desire hasps our lives to rocks and surf,
where we once lay, cradling life
in the other's tongue, sorrow shaky and rotten
inside the hard shell where, transparent and rapt,
we unearthed each other, hemorrhaging all that came
before in blood and feces until the floor softened with it
and we ovulated together, holding love
                    in the mouth of what was.
We slept until the ground soaked up our bodies
and we held on until morning and then dusk
passed and night swallowed us whole, leaving only
a tuft of blue on the spot where we learned to die.

In Paradise Answers Rarely Come

In paradise answers rarely come through the body's excretions.
No one reads the sweat above the lip,
the odor that permutates the hair beneath the arms,
the flakes of skin in the crotch's V,
the leavings and additions to being human.
Only the fallen pick through waste
seeking signs of conduct and desire.
Urine has no place beyond its delicate trails
and the few feet with which its scent binds the air,
an earthly coat of being that the angel cannot imagine.

On A Winter Hillside

Where were you when light dipped below,
Your bells ringing only when the coffins came?

Do not turn back to what is known.
Follow the tracks into the snow,
to an ancient fire that gleams
between two stones—talismans
of lives not freely given falling
and lifting before you on creases
of memory you've secured to dream.
Wait by the stones for the sun to set, winter to come,
to know what floats around this thinness close to your lives—

If you listen, as the sun crosses the crest
and light darkens in your eyes, you can hear
us sing, "Unearth our bodies. Bring your shovels,
your ropes, and burlap bags to bind our remains. Pull us
home."

Hear our calling. Close your eyes.
The cold will strike.
Our empty bones will chime.

Trust

after September 11, 2001

Through the porch glass—a white oak, its ragged bark soft
with moisture after a year of drought. Beyond—
a field, pressed and silent with snow, and a truck, shorn
of its chrome. Lichen shrouds the oak's
thin branches, a cocoon of hair hanging from a twig
like an afterthought. For my friend it seems an ampule
for understanding, to me it circumnavigates what I long
for—
a thaw to reveal the stone from which I might conceive

some shape from what I feel. It doesn't matter
whether the entrance to destiny is found
or imagined—but that my imagination stiffens,
stroking only the treeline of the clearing where we spotted
animal tracks earlier, in the snow—a loose crossing
of deer and raccoon, cougar and bear,
a space in which they gather

sun, feel the wind brush their fur.
I do not mean to delineate what it is animals do—
only my own life at the table in front of the glass
looking out on the oak and the battered truck's
muted grille—a malfeasance in the snow, humming
with fungi and scales of loss.

Yet the clearing did seem a sanctuary from fear,
where people, too, might come to sit and listen
to wind and the breathing under the snow—
as if no harm could come to anything.

Of Roots and Dead Fathers

One longed for air, one digs down
for a quiet the other no longer needs;
it scrolls the edges of buried rocks,
slabs of granite, yards thick
and ample as a whale's hide.
Still, for a time they kiss
in an earthly way, exchanging dirt,
flakings of bark and flesh.

Imagine it to the end, the dismantling
of father. His sketches and blueprints
of apartments and houses and
a graveyard, his plot colored-in
in final control, crinkled under drawings
on his drafting table. The way
his death smile draws
out into wisps of skin
and his thin beard lies
like a mat across his chest,
beetles hauling his disclosed flesh
up to the light.

Light Comes To The Desert

She came to him again, without warning,
as light happens on the desert, not
a moment unattached to what came before
or after. That she came shyly was enough,
her nostrils quivering, as if to read
the current that passed between them—fear
or love or simply the closing and opening
of a thought that in itself might inflame
the tableland, needling the roots of the desert

for a language that said, "join me in making beauty."

He watched as she moved in the room,
lucent and sure, a blanket of sun at her feet,
before she vanished. He felt her in the misty
leaves of the cottonwood, peering down
at the road he walked upon.

Silent Confession To A Catholic Student

Know your bones, he said to her,
a young woman fidgeting with buttons
and sighing as he quietly read her poems.
The professor had too often invoked Thoreau's dictum
as a kind of Eucharist for himself.
When he lifted his eyes to her, he saw
she'd cloistered who she was in a glass-blue coyness
that tempted him as sea cliffs tempt so many to step
into mystery. Too often he had
climbed into pines and waited
for the wind to take his confession,
burrow it back into his pores. What chance
here to uncloak her nouns and verbs, pour
the chalice wine into her letters
so that they gleamed red?

He spoke about woods and breaking
time down, cracking ice
with rocks until the sluggish creek
filtered into new channels and surged
under the membrane. He saw a new
expression gathering in her face:
that she gravitated to the way he dredged
her words as if the little she'd given him
were tea leaves transfigured into sacraments.
If he peeled away her contacts,
would it be passion streaming down her cheeks
or tears scented with lily of the valley.
He realized then he had no place
bearing the chasuble of the confessional.

When she left the office, this station
of respect he'd finally breached
into being, he looked down at her poems
in his lap and knew she felt more clearly
than he the breastbone of life, that she'd
found a voice and he had coerced what he could
not know into the rectory of his own wishes.
He could not run after her, explain
to her bowed head, her flushed skin,
could not place his apologetic hands
on her young shoulders.

He wanted to confess his desire
for all things beautiful, how he believed our cells
ached to touch another, the invisible vestibule
between us that erases need.
Surely, he would never
know his bones, the canon of his story
spread thin across the plains and hills,
the tendon sheathed
in the undergrowth where he would not go.

The professor stood in the doorway, the trail
of her going swelling the hall,
the way truth cantilevers one's life
and something inside pulls back in fright.

Layout Artist

He left his desk, papers strewn
like blown leaves, cursor pulsing,
to unbind his mind, his body bound by pixels
and points, eyes burnt
with after-images of guitars and mics,
drums and amps stamped
into paper, a flat and spaceless music
he carried with him as he walked
the halls, shaking fatigue's
inky notes from his fingers.

Through a field riven by thorn and bone,
along Bear Creek, where herons
once hunted, humped over the water
like old men on street corners searching for coins,
past shopping carts and bags nested in reeds,
and a weathered woman on a cooler who blessed him
as he went. He walked to exorcise the sounds
that tortured his ears like strings of memory
never achieving form. He went as far as he could get
into the dark green way, where in tamarisk song
sparrows rattled and coyote-jawed dropouts swayed
and smoked their way to heaven.

To unbind his weary eyes, he rested beneath
a cottonwood listening to the toothless clapping
of old leaves, directing, "that way, go that way."
The homeless woman had long disappeared
into the brush. Robins hopped from branch to branch
of low trees like quarter notes looking for wholeness.

His cubemates would be playing a final game
of "Find My Pulse," before tidying their desks
        and heading home.

"Here I am," he said. And went into a blind
of blackberries, emerged in a clearing
where a vagrant's fire sputtered, its thin line
of smoke giving shape to winter's composition.
He knelt, pulled something from the ash,
held it, pulsing, in his palms, a fledgling heat.
He could either breathe into it or return it.
On the ground, next to the fire, he laid himself out,
looked up through branches to the sky, held his breath,
a scattering of low clouds to the west beginning to color, the
        harmony
of freeway and creek surging when he closed his eyes.

Daily Coffee

Cockeyed and crosswise:
a table, a chair pushed back; the café's
owner lifts it, tucks it
into place; one arm braced
on the chair back, he bends—
like a ballerina on one leg, stalking grace, the other
raised behind parallel to the striped and filthy carpet—
and sweeps up a fallen napkin; this his gift of order
to a room already spacious from leavings:
mothers and toddlers, students and teachers rumbling
through texts and papers, tarot readers and the hopeful:
the air now, the sippings, the chewings, the swallowings,
everything that breathes open to the threaty rasps
of old guys who congregate
mornings to crab:

government's inept, kids grouse
too much, ruffling their feathers, pecking at lice
grown too large for their beaks, Jesus,
the public's too stupid to vote;
on and on they go, and when they're done
they turn back to their papers, smacking lips,
and clicking tongues, sighing and shaking
their heads at the stable of news; then they start again, a
                litany
that draws in the room: with age, they mourn, organs shift
and toddle like drunken toys, prattle on
in the drums of their bodies, carrying on too often,
on separate orders, "from whence I don't know,"
these blasted quotidian snares

lapsing with age; "better to ignore the terror
of it all, the gimpy bowels and sputtering hearts,
say they're the Milky Way stationed in the imagination.
It's the only way to go." For emphasis, one guy screws
a napkin into his empty mug, as if with twisting he might screw
himself backwards into wholeness,
the dirty napkin at the bottom an embryonic message
hidden from everyday use. "Otherwise,"
another wisely concludes, "we'd be flinging ourselves
                       around here
like flies triangulating the room in an attempt to trap
something without motion, turn it to stone maybe so
that we can breathe without fearing the intake
of breath or its withdrawal."

I listen fascinated. These bent backs, filmy eyes
and hapless limbs beating against the room's tightening skin
                       the song
of what it means to be dying. But who else should know? Not I,
who in youth embraced the idea of slow decay
as metaphor for something more, an existential exit into what
I no longer know. For them the metaphor is all.
At mid-life I keep my balance with worlds
more mundane than theirs; the relationships that
distract me from my body are the sluice that guides
me away from those interior shiftings—the kisses
of my wife, the glories of my boys, the way the sun strokes
the decking and yes, even
the drooping of our dog who in blindness
bumps into a wall, and then, as if he's been slapped,
humps his back and drops his head, snaking it
along the floor, so that he has to stare up at the world.

Elegy To My Father

please don't try to save me, he said, it makes me nervous

He found himself dipping ever more into darkness
his life a fine trail along the river he now traveled.
He did not move toward God,
but against the fear of trembling. He saw his paling life
and determined to compose his dying.
When he found himself in our company
he smiled in his cheerful way, the pain a private thing
he would not have us know until there was no not knowing.
He sang in his pain and when he could no longer sing
he high-tapped his hand on his thigh, his fingers calling
for spirit and memory; we organized ourselves
around our father. We sang the songs
he taught us; we sang as if we too
might leave this place, rise up with him,
into some vortex where consciousness was the sound
of us and his fingers rising
and falling to "Row Row Row Your Boat
Gently Down the Stream" and
"Those Were the Days My Friend."
That we were there was our gift.
That he sang with us was his. He moved along
bending low in the river, as the waters within
him swelled and carried him on
to another pool. Death is what he wanted.
His life now a diffused shadow that drifted about him
like some fisherman's horrible net drawing him up
once upon once, again and again into the air
where he choked and spluttered, until finally
he jumped the net and swam quickly
into the death waters.
That was the end.

Borrowed Fire
(A Love Story)

When he returned, sunlight
broke in violet lakes
around his ankles and knees.
He lay on on the carpet by the sliding glass door,
beauty and simplicity hewed
from desert air stinging his lungs.
He followed loping fields to the blackberries
and cottonwoods at Meyer Creek,
where light flicked back
to the afternoon, crossed to an upslope
of farmland and the town
across the valley, then into the forested hills
above it, his body seizing,
as if to wrench free some nut
that banged in his belly.

He knew grief as a kind of gratitude
that could not be fully riven
from flesh or organs —
for he had not cried like this for decades
since the woman he loved left.
He'd waited, knowing that if she didn't return
something more than loss would inhabit
him. It was an exquisite torture
that would wail for years at the end of every
kiss and breath; or in the abrupt reprieve
of her return, which would forge him
to her as a dying creature claimed
by the mud that preserves it.

Weeks later, the sunbursts in his joints
have deepened into the purple of afterbirth,
scattering the desert heat in streaks and bowls
of pink and yellow, across triceps and thighs
and calves, like patches of flowers on a hillside.
Yet, the heat he anchored too close to bone
still grows, like an absorbent firestone:
when he touches his skin
it burns like a lit match held too close;
it collects in his feet and flames from his toes,
this fever released and replenished,
a grief for all things turned
in the black arteries of memory.

After the Trees Came Down

He awoke in the night to slugs of wind,
his heart its first victim, ramming
his chest, still unsteady in dream,

the ghost poplar's great limbs
cracking above their bed, their bodies crossed,
touched by fate, the ceiling crunch, the casket
weight, darkness . . .

then understanding and peace, listening
to the breathing world—

wind-born sockets of air, thick firs
flipping their wings, the single yew
that persisted beside the pumphouse

flying, the red cedars' pliable
branches built to accommodate what will come . . .

Breath

In this moment I am held
all the love and anger, beauty and fear in me
are welled

in the faint mustiness of exposed roots by a stream.

This moment, this breath catches on the patterns of our lives
like light on rocks, bright contours of being,

the expanding circle of a stone cast into water.

If we are still long enough
the stone will drop, the wellstone of our beings
sinking to the untouched source of breath.

There is nothing to be afraid of.
It is only what we have done always,
a fair exchange of ever-growing life and death within.

I breathe into the present
and the future is born, a hesitant and bereaved thing
longing for what came before, and then it is gone,

as quiet in its passing as any stream.

Mountain Artery

How odd to sit in an artery
where winter's waters once gushed,
another displaced stone popping
from the arterial wall,
the lapping trees across the ravine
reminders of unsteadiness, the granite
boulders to either side,
organs of a mild season after deep
precipitation, accepting blankly,
like parents, wind and sky and rain,
while he, strange rock, too quickly
                disappearing,
feels wings from above sweep through him,
the dizzying knowledge of emptiness and desire

The Flood

I
The boy kneels by the river and cannot drink.
Fish float, infused with scum.
Deer and raccoon find solace in the soft mud,
their stiff bodies prayers to the unknown.
"This cannot be," he thinks, and stands,
fingernails in his thigh. He will not leave.
Blood dries and cracks along his warm calf. He senses storms,
the concentration of airstreams around the globe,
the electricity of stasis, scatterings of the bloated.
He knows there is nothing anywhere.

II
"This cannot be," he says.
Wild, he goes from place to place,
shakes the strong frames of houses.
"What have we done, what have we done?"
His father reaches for him. "Quiet son. Let the people be."

III
The boy stands in the wheatfield weeping.
The bright midwest sun gleaned in the yellow stalks.
The heat in his limbs.
He cannot believe how powerful he is and weeps again.
The shimmering wheat, the low hills, his name.
They are everywhere.

Where We Stand

I want to take you with me,
erase the fractures and tend
again a garden planted
with unknown seeds, to wait
for summer, when we unearth
the shy flames of discord.

I cannot shed the weapons
I have wrought, cannot clip
the limbs that balance
me—but I can be a brace
against the rapids that plunge
around you, I can be a bridge

for you to walk across; look down
into the river and you will see
the patterns of trees, the shadows
of leaves, the form of my love for you.

Do not fold yourself into the crib
of ice cast in the rocks
at the headwaters;
it holds nothing but sorrow—
a rote student of the past
frozen at the edge of our lives.

I want to rise from the base
of the gorge, extend up to you,
your reflection rippling
on the surface, because I love you
and I am drawing enough water
to hold us both a long time.

Dido's Tears

The inward fire eats the soft marrow away and the internal wound bleeds on in silence. Virgil, *The Aeneid*, bk IV; l. 93

A god from heaven's high air is goading me to hasten our break away, to cut the cables. Virgil, *The Aeneid*, bk IV; l. 798

His wife was right, the mirror paraded a sameness
between them that had shadowed their years,
from the first night pressed into the cliff
while a storm bled itself in the sea
and they'd taken refuge in each other's dreams.
He'd spent their years feeding on the horizon's glow,
his future quivering there like a blind waiting to be raised,
but that hunger was drawn from his body as the bloodflow
from Carthage. Now they shared eyes sheltered
by too much skin, sagging breasts and a belly
that slumped over his belt like a sack of grain.
He swiveled in his chair. Out the window: cherry
trees pampered into bloom by a false spring,
his wife lopping the shriveled buds
off last year's roses. There was something torturous
about the light that stroked her face, an archeology
he would not touch for fear his fingers would expose
a soil tilled with tears so caustic nothing could grow from it.
"I love you," he apologized later, putting a hand
                to her cheek.
She nodded and turned to undress for bed; he studied
the smooth part under her arms as she pulled
                up the black blouse
salted with crumbs he'd been too shy to brush away.
 "How soft your hair is," he said. He bound
his arms around her, her breasts in his palms,
weighty with a hope he'd long ago abandoned.

As he held her, he thought of all the wrongs committed
in the name of longing, how he had held himself in check
always, for a land he could not see. He thought of the sailors
down at the harbor, strapping themselves to posts
for a coming squall, their legs dangling over the pier,
half-blinded by the glint of salt where the sea had been.

Cohabitation
(In Other Words, Love)

He didn't know how to help her
or how he had come to be
in these falls of blood and air.
When she'd cried, he'd chosen
to form within her, the lub and dup
of her heart, pumping and hissing,
the rumbles and rasps
easily adopting the guilt
forged along the viscera
of his travels. He had found balance
with her help, had put his cheek
to her warm breastbone and listened,
at moments a revelation
of pulse, at others a wave
that wouldn't break, as though her life
were lived in abeyance and that it was he
she waited for.

He imagined her form, the slope
of her nose, the dark skin, eyes,
the smoothness of her movement,
the quiet, how he rocked
in her presence. How he longed to run
his fingers along her sides.
He thought, there must be a way,
And called to her. "Let me out. I'm coming out,"
felt her hands move under her belly,
the slight uplift in the way mothers cradle a foetus,
that imagining growing in the womb.
This was how she chose to hear him.

He wouldn't force himself unwanted
through her canals, that pain too close to bear.
He settled in her belly, breathing her air,
drinking her waters, believing one day
she would open her chest,
that they would embrace
his freedom together.

Of Breath and Mirrors

And now?
        She turns away
from the breeze, the sea,
        the desert
that tries to bloom in her gut,

to a wall—
        somewhere within
a sweet odor of paint—
        to seize her indifference.

What shall she do?
        Fold up
like a spider in the shower,
        accept the fumes
that drench her body,
        embrace her death?

Press harder, into the wall
        until it unleashes
a flight of seed, the binding sea;
        press until pain
triumphs, releases, the cartilage
        twisting, breaking,

the dry bones of memory laid
        in a desert mortuary
or his hand pressed to her wrist
        while he sleeps—
the confidence of unconsciousness.

There is no logic outside
        this moment, no contract
greater than intake and outtake,
        no intimacy
greater than the tenuous breath

distilled on the shower's mirror,
        that she might see
what she is and where she has been,
        arouse the world behind her.

Untitled

The ache and twist of endurance—
a life chosen in the wake of honesty,
its waves racing after, then buckling,
and flattening into a plain of water,
mixed with casts of cloud and earth.
It was once so easy. I turned to track
the waves behind, the crests' fall,
the white water curls so fragile,
a childhood there struggling to survive.
I thought I held it, my body the cradle
for a river I would always roam.

Too much. Too much, the roil and spike
of words. Instead turn forward. Take
refuge in a bog around a bend,
the shadows thick with reed
and cattail, their frayed yellow heads
signals for the coming heat,
the burnishing of hills and clear
skies I can long find beauty in.

Yet remember, the arced trills and scratchy peeps
of redwing blackbirds, their dance
of color and song, the opened limbs
and bodies of the yellow water iris are always
reminders of the fragility relinquished.

Treatise On Emptiness
after Adam Zagajewski

I would be no different from rocks
their ancient heads at rest on the desert,
the crisscross of living evaporating into the sands
as a rainbow vanishes with a shift in stance.

All flesh would conform to skin, follicles of hair
would sift the air for slashes of color
no draft straining between marrow and stone.

For I will be the mountain, the red rock, the plains,
no longer acknowledging the boundaries of nerves.
I will be the twilled heart of man
        and sycamore
                white
                        as bone.

The Verdict

> *What terrible sin:*
> *could their souls have committed*
> *that their lives in this world should begin with a verdict:*
> *you are sentenced to life.*
> *With no possibility of parole.*
> —Yehuda Amichai, from "Israeli Travel:
> Otherness is All, Otherness is Love"

Do you know where you walk?
between creek and wood, steel,
      too, and screws,
what we use   rusty   you'd best run
        to cross the rotted beams
cross here,
            cross now,
a popping and creaking
      ships sinking
where we've been,

      falling…
Hold my hand. Bless me. It's all disappearing—
we captured so much before

                          they came
            Mothers   fathers
Bless me—winding in—
recall what you can—there in that sack
a space shifting and rocking   rock-a-bye—
      Sea, the sea, cloven
mountains, at their crown,
the fulcrum, the ship, tipping, the sea rising … goodbye
      the mast fluttering … sea rising   our mothers
rocking, the demons coming
"You want too much," they said.

The verdict…
Can't you hear? Listen,
Can't you bear what all bear?
  Before   collapse   —   a bridge,
an air, a sea, a ship — hold your breath
There.
       Hold.
                        Long
Breath. Breathing
Breathing.   The way we do
when we feel it come.
Breathing   breathing
     So still   the body
under the bridge
     when it falls

Myth

When the heron came
its crooked neck
a gray root in the bank
bared its broad wings
and stepped from its cast, craned
over the roiling
creek, I thought of the miraculous
grace a moment
when time falls
our first duty to the glint
                      upstream

A Girl's White Socks

It's easy to settle down by a river,
gather needles, twigs, and sticks
to start a fire, be quiet into the night
before the mind begins to stir
like fish rising in early morning,
then strike, remorse
hacking away at the banks,
as if you, might have saved
the young girl, her white socks
filled with leaves, balanced
in a maple tree, open
to the steady flow of couples
below flirting with coitus
or final years, their deaths
hanging in rings from their ears.
You believe the black and worn
soles of her socks
are testaments to walking
until you can no longer bear
knowing that to go on is everything,
her small voice so soft in the air,
pleading to passersby.
The fire crackles. You tend it,
promising those who die young
to spread your fingers in the water,
work them like gills until the bones numb,
promise to visit their graves, to remember
that lingering distresses are merely turns
in the river, and that currents
will always stir something new
from the river's bottom.

Summer Winds

Few people know themselves well.

For example, when I glance
in a mirror I see a fallen master,
[genes that once flexed in the surreal
tucked into sheaths of backorders.]

Others describe a muscly man
who embeds broad logs
along a stream to weather erosion.

My wife sees a boy weeping when a raven
lifts from a lamppost and flies over his car.

If I knew how to turn in the right direction
I would head uphill into the fires
if only to save myself from the negligence

I've perpetrated on the world.

Summer Winds 2

When the winds come
the lonely lie happily on rooftops.
They're often blown
overboard into night.

At least they've learned
what it means to die in motion.

Others lie in fields of tall grasses
to watch them arc like wedding arbors
across the tamped sheaves of their bodies.

When the world folds over them
they will unsheathe their old skins.

I like to walk among lanky cottonwoods
swaying in the winter sky
to remember when life was flexible as a living tree.

My sons stand firm and graceful in strong storms.
One day I hope they learn happiness.

The Bird's Wish

The sun comes up
in a small hand
opening the huge door
of the parent's bedroom—
the dark panting of night
floods the house and the child's
struck face—school books drop
like empty baskets.
Fear pulses in their bodies
as the woman shakes loose
and the man buries his head / himself
in "good morning" and "come here,"
welcoming the child to bed
where love still circulates
like fresh baked bread, its aroma
feathery and semi-sweet. The man cannot help
himself, puts his hand between the woman's legs
as the child burrows, small coyote—
her legs merciless
the fabric of love
replaced by the dark vault of wishes.

On the Bank of a Desert

A river surges onto the bank of a desert
where yellow bell flowers coil up stiff blades

A white cat rises, shakes sand from fur, gazes
at the hushed knocking of flowers,
the sun flare in steel

Listen, to the rustle of brown sticks
and leaves in a crook of rock blown there by desert
winds from an elm across the river, where a man sits
hugging his knees, a T-shirt clinging
to body sweat, the hairs of his chest a fine mat
through this translucency

He is crying
Notice the tongue flick out
to pull the tear in

His father has died
This man will die

He watches the cat stand, can almost see sand and dust
fly out from its white fur, feels the sting of the absolute
unleashed in the swell of a dust devil. He waits
for the sword to fall, the sun to soften,
the cat to lie back down on the desert

Hear his breath,
the rise and fall of his chest,
the letting go

Pilot Light

I spend mornings shadowing
                    the pilot
light; it flickers against the heat
          stone; the flame bows
and drifts one way,
                    then another,
from a wind of its own shaping.
Sometimes I turn up the thermostat.
The heating element blazes
          clarifying the carnelian underside
of the curved stone—
it glows like rock arches
at sunset, or a campfire
                  as night falls.

I'm invited to sit and listen
among the broad-faced peoples
of the desert, to stories
                  of how, in the morning,
in veins of trees, the world
glistens, and blushes along the rims
where jackrabbits stand up to acknowledge
                    beginnings and ends.

When the wine is done,
we rouse. The black night
opens its hearth, a fleck of moon funneling us
up the slope to our tents, their entrances
                    facing northeast where ridgelight
          breaks from darkness
to reveal the fluted sky

we must all climb if we are to go
                forward from absence
into the harsh light of summer.

It is then, hidden things disclose
themselves, insects begin to hum,
and the black-spotted
                lichen, that rings
    the flats of rocks become a map
to the labyrinth we spend our lives
seeking entrance to.

We mumble goodnight.
I close the tent flap.
My friends have put away
                their azure and turquoise,
settled into their beds as I will do,
our lives linked by more than story
or shared blankets, the stutter-steps
                of our dreams arcing
into the course of the river,
tracing natural cairns
to a shore where there is no longer any need
                to cry out to one another.

Chamber of the Oracle

She looks down and across the gulch at the wide berth saguaros give each other, like the Indians of this country, their trailers and small houses dotting the sageland north of black canyon country, shallow-rooted hard desert plumes soldered to the molten crust to brace against the arid fingers of the city luring them south.

Here, even the charcoal bush, its seven-fingered stems, which, although almost dead, the harsh land allows to return self-contained into the soil. Here the unnamed tiniest flowers, their eighth-inch pink and white blooms secure under the uneven shade of slate, fan the flap of her hot brain and rolled sleeves. And here the pink hairs of owl clover, a ciliated bloom like dandelion ready to lift off from its yellow history to cross invisible airwaves to another land.

The sun bolts to the stems of even hidden things.

The shadowland's plumage of cactus and desert featherdusters grafts a new understanding of green and brown that remains nameless in her body.

Across the narrow arroyo, her friend, so worried earlier about catching a flight, has melted in the orange-blossomed ocotillo and cholla, his heart sweating heavily with anticipation through the purple cotton stripes blooming on his back, his entire body beating now as a fine heat bears down and he becomes almost indistinguishable from the stones.

She has found peace sheltered in a country of survivors, resting against a sling of slate knives, Mesozoic shields that have sliced through the stiff crust, laying open the land.

She wants to lie face down on this earth, stretch her body in all directions, take the imprint of stone and stems into her skin, to hold what she can.

Guest of Honor

When the cat cries at the sliding glass door
we turn in unison.
There's nothing there but the chipped deck
and rail, a husky light brimming in the maples
and the reflection of the table where we're frozen,
like figures in a Franz Hals, goblets raised, the unease
in our minds not yet captured in the glass.
Conversation continues, the bottle
passed around again, another serving
of spaghetti. In candlelight,
the long noodles quiver in their bowls, then settle
into place. A woman picks a fallen
lettuce leaf from the carpet,
tucks it under her bread plate. "I'm so tired,
worn out," another says, and begins the story
of his latest firing. "When I was young
and free," another interrupts, and we laugh.
"When I was young," he starts again,
"around the time of Woodstock,
I got lost in the woods. I was thirteen.
They sent a rescue party to find me."
He raises his head, smiles, sips his wine,
peers at each of us, even the drunk one who lies
on the couch. We listen
to the click of fork tines
and porcelain, like brittle leaves,
a wind. "And?" the eldest
among us asks. "I'm still lost, but
nobody's looking for me any more."
I hear the cry, turn again, everyone
follows my eyes. We stare,

a moment, at ourselves in the glass
looking back at us. "Certainly," the guest
of honor says, "it must be ourselves we hear
begging to be let in."

Elegy for Aryeh

The day you died,
the day folded back without a name

I arrived here in the dark,
a crystal fog flittering in my headlights,
luminous as that day
along the lakeshore in the fall,
when together we walked into holiness.
In the dark morning,
I opened the door to possibility,
imagining a life briefer than my own,
a place where sons must turn to each other
instead of to their father,
where song no longer breathes
in your lungs or lifts from your tongue,

but rises from the mouths of others.

In mourning, I turned the lights off,
closed the car door, waited in the dark.
Crystals fell collecting
in a white dust around me.
I knelt to retrieve them—
these still and quiet things
that eluded me while you lived,
dissolved now at my touch
and formed a pool
of understanding in my body.

Oh my fierce and gentle brother, I will draw
water for you from this fog, these fragile wings.

I will hold the water in my palms
for others to drink.
To this deep and abiding well
you have built within me,
I will return
again and again.

Kindness
January 12, 2 a.m

When kindness
is abandoned
for the sake of honesty
the doubt
that exists within all bonds
may open to embrace one's friends
and close behind them,
their memories left
in outlines on the floors.

Plato may have slept with truth
but when his heart
began to fail at a wedding feast,
he welcomed friends and strangers
to soothe his mortal fears

I once told a friend
we were friends no longer
for he had too long hidden
in a life of show,
casting a mindless line
into barren waters.

When I find myself
standing in the river's dark shallows
a stranger in the world
I, too, may yet learn kindness.

Fertile Ground

Daily the dead
        visit
a stark interference

opened mouths
stiffened
and contorted fingers
        no longer

reaching anywhere.

The hills' barren flanks
        are calm as sleeping cats
the rivers
        gray with stubble
the deck stairs brittle
        as grasshoppers

and the flames that stretch
        from house to house
are reminders only:

Time is a gap-toothed child
and we bury
what we know
in fertile ground

Another Story

In another story, the boy grew up.
He had lost his bow, but its memory
clung to his muscles.
At night his arms twitched
and he dreamed of spiders
spinning their own wind.
When he woke, stars
had broken through the sky,
the ice had retreated into the road.

Hope

His wife holds out hope. He takes
the blossom, kneads
its silky body between thumb
and index, supplant
its identity with fingerprints,
as he has held
everything before him, first
kisses and births,
the preludes and arias that brought
their children to sing and mark
his darkness with song.

Their mother quiet now in dream, steps
across cracks
and tree roots while he runs
his hands along the window ledge
and blows on the hundreds of little flies
silent in left over webs,
the tiny half-hearts
of their wings fluttering.

The Choice

When you whisper into pillows
too long, you will become silent;
whisper into wind, you will become
a funnel for voices long-sheathed in air.

Either way, you lose. Whether
placid as dusk's tenuous light
or voracious as dawn, the past
will relocate your dreams.

Your ears may turn inward,
listing toward a sea break;
your mind, unraveling on a shore,
may turn spongy as blankets of sea grass.

Or you may cast a net into a canyon,
gathering the world's fish on your deck.
What will you do with all the noise?
Whichever way you turn, there is pain.

You have only one choice.
Whisper into the tidal waters;
anemones and urchins will be
the vessels that carry you home.

We Are Built Of Light

We are built of light. We shy from this.
The isolation of acknowledgment is more than we can bear.
We share this secret that we cannot speak,
to each other or anyone. We kiss in corners
where it is dark as if this might help. We tell our dreams
and pretend all dreams are fictions. People like us
and have us over; we eat together and tell stories,
sometimes about the light of our past.
Always, it is the past that circles us,
that we touch and hold for fear
of that which is still light.

Poem

In the desert there are no answers

only beliefs
organization persists
shadowless among the slate

a canyon mesh
circulates and pronounces, fine
as the sweetened breath that slips
from the mouth of a sleeping infant

Nothing can be defined

I sway
when flowers flare from fallen saguaros
my life unbarred among the rocks

when rivers flow through arid plains
I imagine millions of arterial miles
flood life's parched lands

And the skies

What can be sung of their broad arms
What expanses brought to bear on the present

When you smile
the desert's flowers and finely wrought
waters filter through sands
into my veins and bones

my own internal flowers
the heart and liver kidney and spleen
like happy children perk from their sallow folds

When you hold me, my body expands
into a color nameless
as a desert sky arias slipping from my fixed bed
into a vibrant air

giving thanks to this mortal life

Coda

The madrone barks
"red"   the green
       river
cradles the reflection
       its currents
cradling

the madrone's red bark
the green river cradling
       a cousin's reflection

cradles the dust
         a reflection
    an echo

       to follow
  come   with me

  come down
the sad creek's lane

pries at its lines
at its confines and shape
     pries at its branches
pries at its branches
        pries at its leaves
its current's insistence   its itches
    and pleases
bites at its sleeves
       pulls
at bodies asleep
    sifts

through our bodies while we sleep
   bends and binds
      deliberates and heeds
the shallows
        deflecting
   reflections
     while there in the deep
chamber of silt
   a shadow
in the
   chamber
      of silt
and stone
a bleached shadow rests
   waits
      teases the confines of shape
its wind a hollow
   it bends
     the tree's vulnerability
   its leaves
teases as time leaches
   bodies asleep

the madrone
   stripped green
       new
its skin
       stripped

let go
let go
I'll gather you deep
in my arms
when you go.

www.ingramcontent.com/pod-product-compliance
Lightning Source LLC
Chambersburg PA
CBHW020130130526
44591CB00032B/583